# JUST JOKING

## OVER 300 JOKES INSIDE!

camp quality.

laughter is the best medicine.

SCHOLASTIC
SYDNEY AUCKLAND NEW YORK TORONTO LONDON MEXICO CITY
NEW DELHI HONG KONG BUENOS AIRES PUERTO RICO

Scholastic Australia Pty Limited
PO Box 579 Gosford NSW 2250
ABN 11 000 614 577
www.scholastic.com.au

Part of the Scholastic Group
Sydney • Auckland • New York • Toronto • London • Mexico City • New Delhi • Hong Kong • Buenos Aires • Puerto Rico

Published by Scholastic Australia in 2013.

Text and illustrations by Dan McGuiness.



---

National Library of Australia Cataloguing-in-Publication entry
Title: Just Joking / by Dan McGuiness.
ISBN: 9781742837352 (pbk.)
Target Audience: For primary school age.
Subjects: Australian wit and humour - Juvenile humour.
Australia - Juvenile humour.
Other Authors/Contributors: McGuiness, Dan.
Dewey Number: A828.402

---

Typeset in Boopee, Hank, Corky, Chicken Scratch, American Typwriter and Bradybunch Remastered.

Printed by McPherson's Printing Group, Maryborough, VIC.
Scholastic Australia's policy, in association with McPherson's Printing Group, is to use papers that are renewable and made efficiently from wood grown in sustainable forests, so as to minimise its environmental footprint.

10 9 8 7 6 5 4 3 2 1 13 14 15 16 17 / 1

# FOREWORD

A wise doctor once said the best way to make a parent laugh is to tickle the child, and that's exactly what Camp Quality does.

At Camp Quality we live and breathe our motto, 'Laughter is the best medicine' everyday, not because we have to but because it's good for us. Research clearly shows that laughter decreases stress hormones, increases immune cells and infection-fighting antibodies, thus improving your resistance to disease. Laughter also increases your heart rate, oxygen consumption, helps with blood pressure and works the muscles in your face and stomach. It's simply a wonderful tool that enhances our life —and what's more it's free!

This hilarious joke book was inspired by Daniel Staunton, one of our Camp Quality kids with an inoperable brain tumour, in 2006. Seven years on, Daniel is still bringing optimism and happiness to other Camp Quality kids, with money from these joke books going towards funding our different programs.

Thanks for believing that laughter is the best medicine!

PHOTOGRAPH BY TIM BAUER.

**Simon Rountree**
**CEO Camp Quality**

P.S. Make laughter the best medicine and tell us your favourite joke! Visit *campquality.org.au/yourjoke* or see the back of this book!

camp quality.

laughter is the best medicine.

## MEET CAMP QUALITY

Our purpose is to create a better life for every child living with cancer in Australia. Whether in hospital, at home, or in school, our programs and services help support these children and their families through the difficult times and onto better days. We passionately practise the power of positive thinking and fun which lead to optimistic and resilient behaviours. It's no wonder we believe that 'Laughter is the best medicine'.

Currently we support one in three children, and through your support we can increase the reach of our programs and services to all children living with cancer.

You'll find that fun and optimism flows through all of our programs, our people and our culture. Please visit our website campquality.org.au and see for yourself why fun, laughter and optimism makes a difference.

# Activities Contents

Q: Where do triceratops sit?

A: **On their tricerabottoms!**

Q: What do bananas do when they get sunburnt?

A: **They peel!**

Q:Which side of a magpie has the most feathers? A:The outside.

**Q:** What happens if you throw a blue hat into the Red Sea?

**A:** It gets wet.

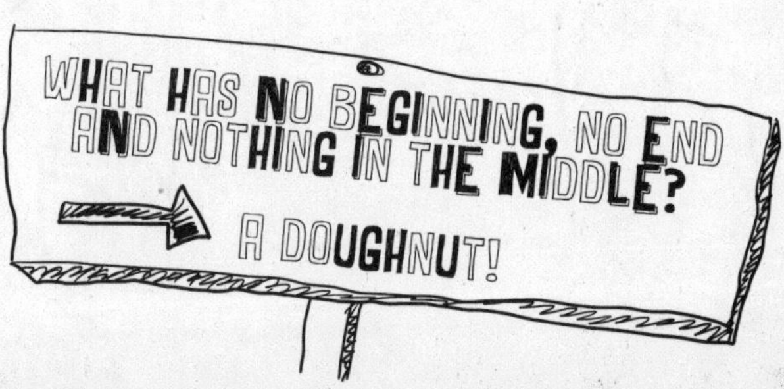

Q: Why did the boat shop go out of business?

A: Everything was always on sail.

Q: What's blue and looks like the sky?

A: The sky.

WHY DID THE ESKIMO GO TO THE DENTIST?

HE HAD FROSTBITE.

Q: What sort of phone calls do Eskimos make? A: Cold calls.

Knock, knock!
**Who's there?**
A fireman.
**A fireman who?**
Stop asking questions!
Your house is on fire!!

Why do dogs wag their tails?
**Because nobody else will do it for them.**

Why did the alligator wear a vest?

He wanted to be an investigator!

**Knock, knock!**
Who's there?
**You.**
You who?
**Don't get so excited, it's just me!**

**Q.** What is black and white and red all over?

**A.** A sunburnt Dalmatian.

**Q:** What do you call a skateboarding ant? **A:** Rampant.

What is the best hand to write with?

Neither—it's best to write with a pen!

Why did the cow cross the road?
To get to the udder side.

Q: Did you hear about the little boy who was named after his father?

**A: They called him Dad!**

**What's red and sits at the bottom of the pool?**

A red tractor.

Q: Why did the child study in the airplane?

**A: He wanted a higher education!**

Knock, knock!
**Who's there?**
Who.
**Who who?**
I didn't know you spoke owl!

**Q:** What do you do if you find a green horse?
**A: Put him in a bag until he ripens.**

**Q:** What goes 'Ha, ha, plop!'
**A:** Someone laughing their head off.

**Q:** What goes 'Boo, hoo, splat!'
**A:** Someone crying their eyes out.

What cheese is made backwards?
**EDAM.**

**What runs But never walks?**
water.

What's orange and sounds like a parrot?
**A carrot.**

# Super Hero Mad Lib

**Fill in the blanks!**

If I was a super hero, I would be called the

.................................... [colour] .................................... [animal].

With my super powers I could .................................... [action]

really fast and lift lots of ....................................s. [object]

Whenever I sensed danger I would .................................... [sound]

very loudly, especially if it was my super enemy:

.................................... [fruit or vegetable] .................................... [dad's name].

Part of my super hero costume would be a

.................................... [colour] .................................... [clothing].

**When Does the alphaBet only have 24 letters?**

When U and I aren't there.

What has six wheels and flies?

**A garbage truck.**

Knock, knock!

**Who's there?**

Scott.

**Scott who?**

Scott nothing to do with you!

Q: Why did the bull wear a bell?

**A: Because his horns didn't work.**

WHAT HAPPENS WHEN A FROG'S CAR BREAKS DOWN?

HE GETS TOAD AWAY!

Q: When is a car not a car?

**A: When it turns into a parking lot.**

HOW DID THE THREE FAT ELEPHANTS STANDING TOGETHER UNDER A TINY UMBRELLA MANAGE NOT TO GET WET? **IT WASN'T RAINING.**

Q: What goes black, white, black, white, black, white?

A: A penguin falling down the stairs.

What makes music on your head?

A head band.

WHERE DO LIONS GET THEIR CLOTHES?

JUNGLE SALES.

WHERE SHOULD A 500-KILOGRAM ALIEN GO?

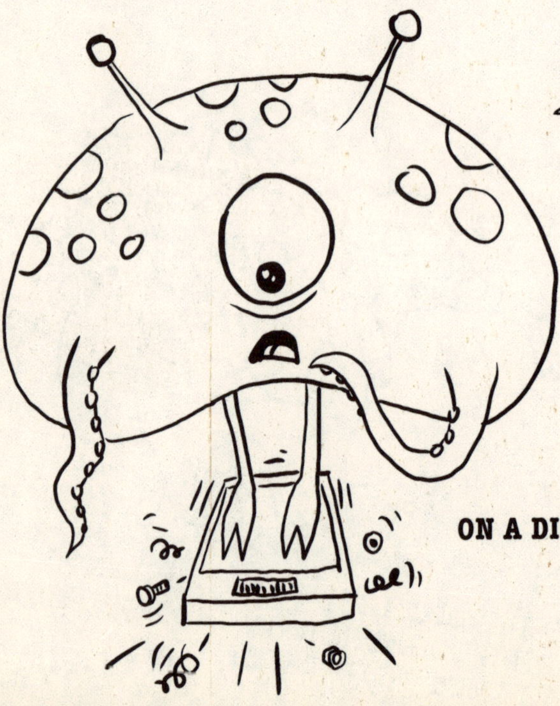

ON A DIET!

**Q:** What's the best way to jump off a really tall ladder without getting hurt?
**A: Jump off the bottom rung.**

What is so fragile that if you say its name you break it?
Silence.

**What would you get if you crossed a vampire and a teacher?**
**Lots of blood tests.**

**Knock, knock!**
Who's there?
**Icy.**
Icy who?
**Icy you through the keyhole.**

What did the mother phone say to the daughter phone?

**Q:** Why did all the kids want to go to the greengrocer?
**A:** He was such a fungi.

You're too young to be engaged.

Why did the cookie go to the doctor? He was feeling really crummy.

Why did the boy take a pencil to bed?
To draw the curtains.

WHY DID THE APPLE WRESTLE WITH THE SAUSAGE ROLL?

THEY WERE HAVING A FOOD FIGHT.

**What's the loudest pet?**
**A trum-pet.**

Q: Why did the toilet run down the hill?

A: To get to the bottom.

WHAT KIND OF TREE FITS IN YOUR HAND?
A PALM TREE.

What do you call a woodpecker with no beak?

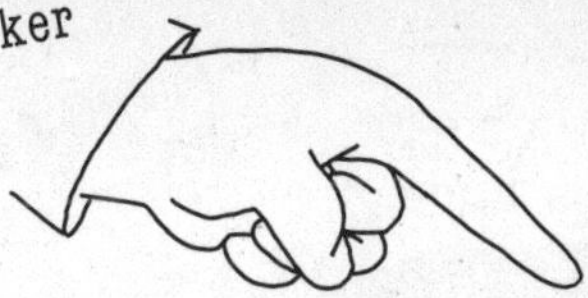

A HEADBANGER.

Q: What do you get when you cross a skunk with a horse?

A: Whinny the pooh!

WHAT'S SMALL, CUDDLY, FURRY AND PURPLE?

**A KITTEN HOLDING ITS BREATH.**

What food are vampires afraid of?
Steak sandwiches.

Q: How does the universe hold up its pants?
A: With an asteroid belt.

WHY DID THE PAINTING GO TO JAIL?
BECAUSE IT WAS FRAMED.

Q: WHEN DOES BOXING DAY COME BEFORE CHRISTMAS DAY?
**A: IN THE DICTIONARY.**

**Why did the bacon laugh?**

Because the egg cracked a yolk.

# SPIDERWEB MAZE

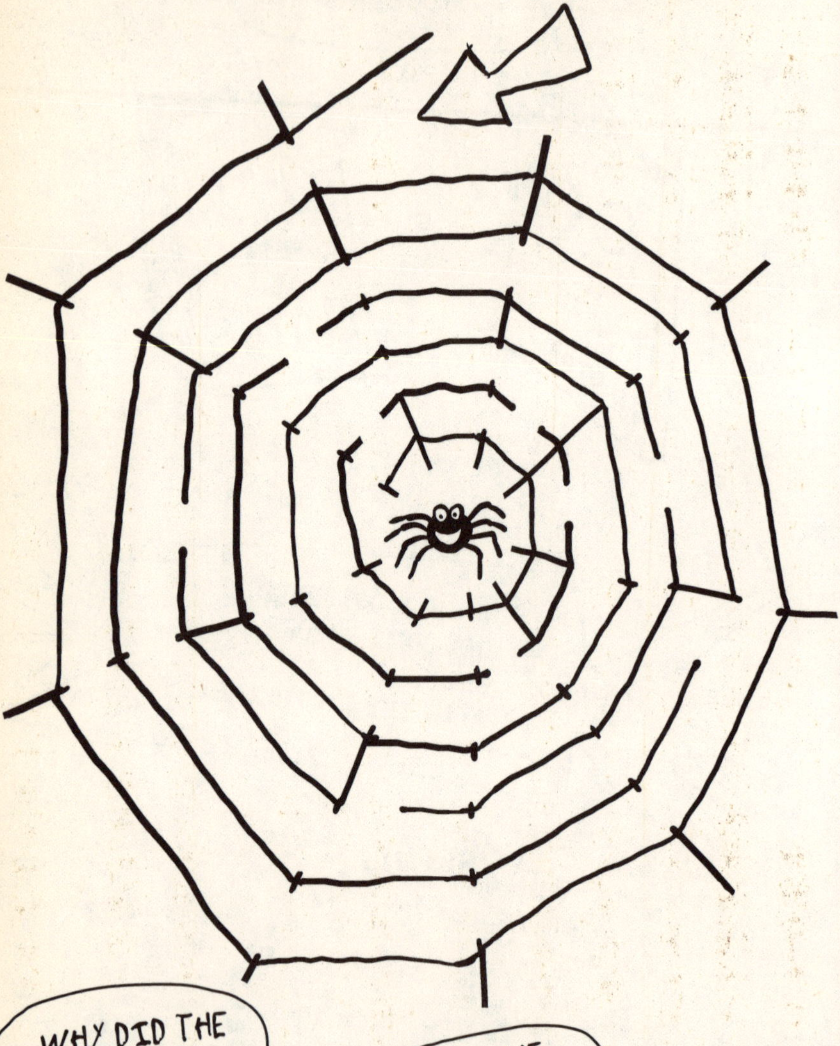

Q: Why did the Cyclops close his school?
**A: Because he only had one pupil.**

WHY DID THE TOMATO GO OUT WITH A PRUNE?
BECAUSE HE COULDN'T FIND A DATE.

WHY DID THE TEACHER GO TO THE BEACH?
**TO TEST THE WATER.**

Q: Where do you find a turtle with no legs? **A: Where you left it.**

What do you call a gorilla with earmuffs on?
**Whatever you want, he can't hear you!**

WHAT DO YOU DO WHEN A DINOSAUR SNEEZES?

GET OUT OF THE WAY!

Who was the bee's favourite rock star?
Sting.

**Q:** What dog can jump higher than a building?
**A:** Any dog, buildings can't jump!

What do you call bears with no ears? **B!**

**Why did the boy eat his homework?**

Because the teacher said it was a piece of cake.

Why did the elephant paint himself different colours?
**So he could hide in the crayon box.**

What's black and white and makes a lot of noise?
A zebra with a drum kit.

NAME TWO ANIMALS THAT LIVE IN A COLD REGION?
**A POLAR BEAR AND HIS WIFE.**

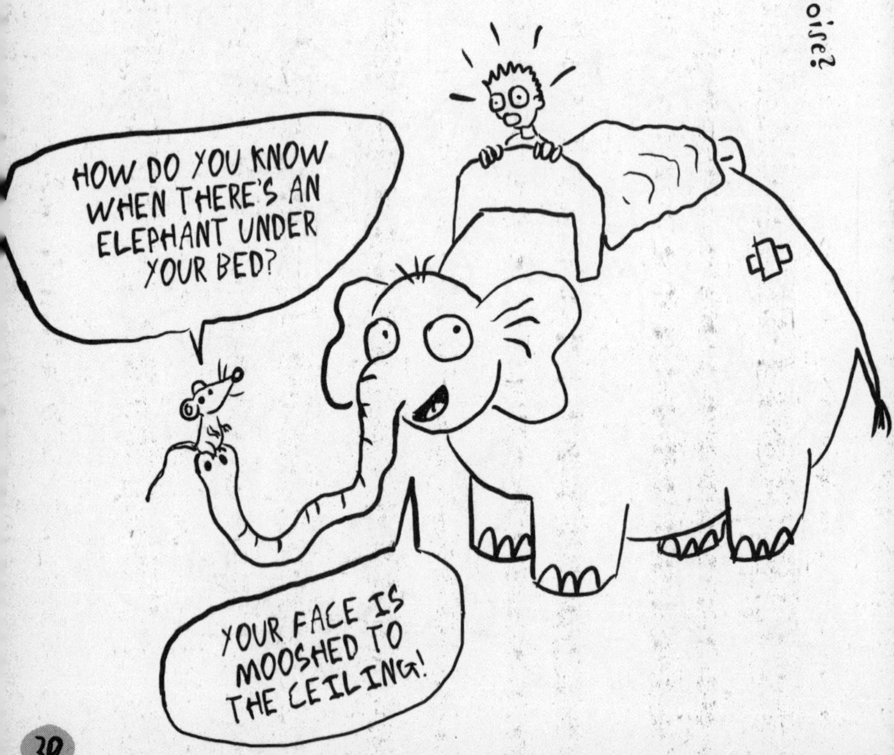

What kind of tricks do rabbits do on a BMX bike?
Bunny hops!

A man walked into bar . . . which broke his nose.

Q: What has four legs but can't walk?

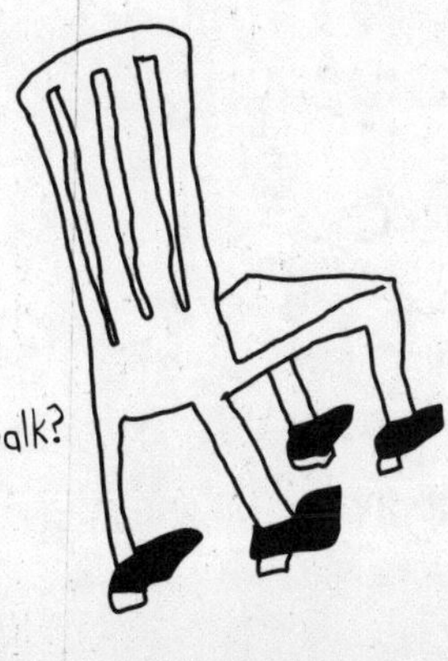

A: A chair.

Q: Where can you find an ocean without water? A: On a map.

WHAT ANIMAL NEEDS TO WEAR A WIG?
**A BALD EAGLE.**

Q: What time do ducks get up in the morning?
**A: At the quack of dawn.**

Have you heard the one about the skunk?
Never mind, it really stinks.

What do you call a bear with no teeth?
A gummy bear.

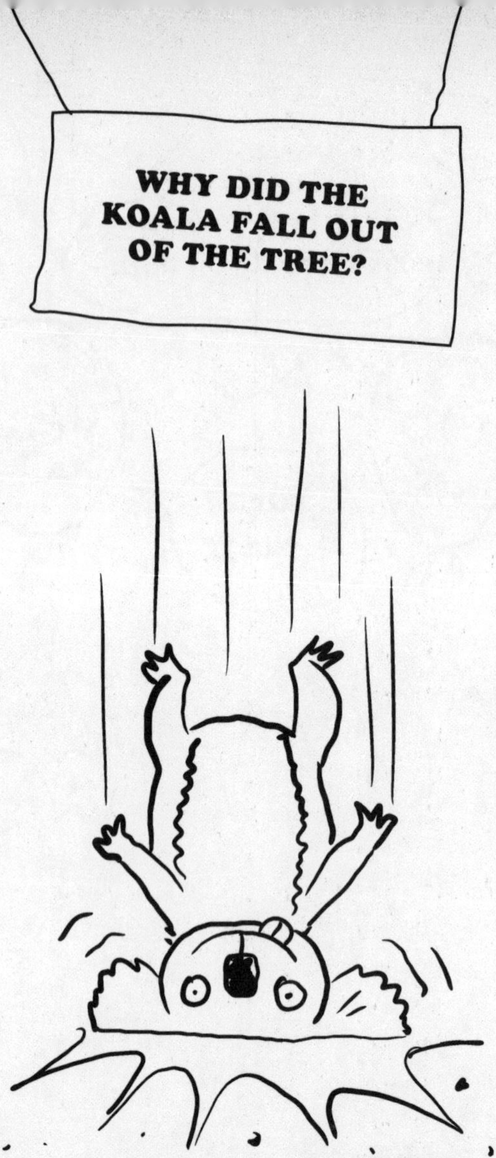


**BECAUSE IT LET GO.**

WHY DID THE OTHER KOALA FALL OUT OF THE TREE?

HE WAS STUCK TO THE FIRST ONE.

**Why did the third koala fall out of the tree?**

He saw the two other koalas doing it and thought it was in fashion.

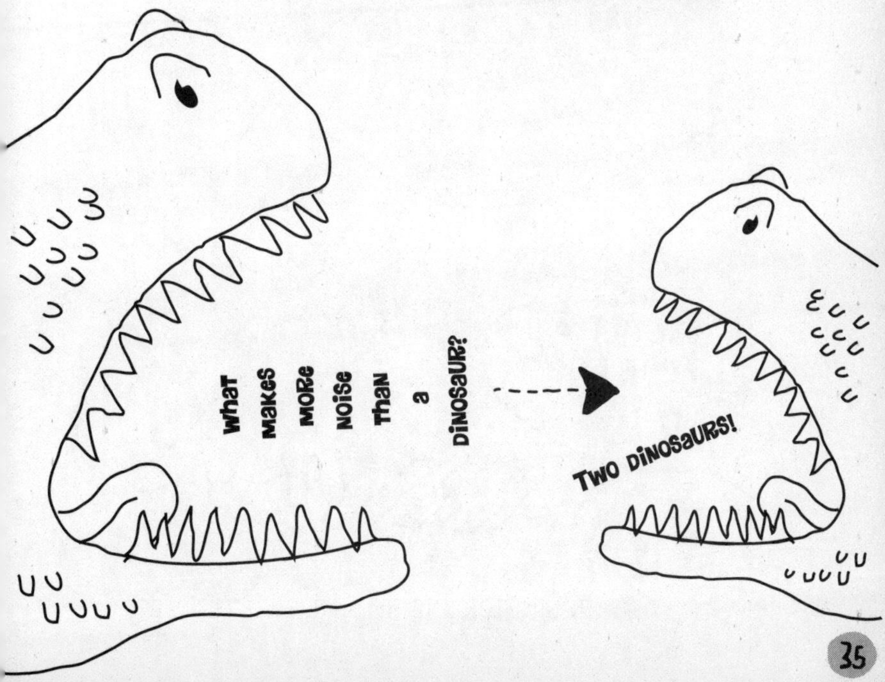

Why was the bum in hospital?
It had a fart attack.

What do you find in a clean nose?
Fingerprints.

**What invention lets you see right through walls?**
**A window.**

**What's green and hangs out of trees?**
Giraffe snot.

What did the carrot say to the cut banana?
Are you peeling OK?

BECAUSE CHICKENS HADN'T EVOLVED YET.

# Cross-the-Road Word Search

E R E H T O N Q R I
O D A F S C L E S W
L N R D I H D O S F
O U D G U I E C K M
C O E F S C S T O P
F R O G C K V W E R
Q G E E D E X Z U R
O Y R T P N E A G Y
W A L K E D S R W H
D L G X H O Z O U W
Z P F W N U C K P O
E P S I V E D I L S
B Q D A O R Y W T B
R K C R O S S I N G
A K E N O E M O S L

chicken
cow
crossing
dinosaur
frog
get
other
playground
road
side
slide
someone
stop
walked
why
zebra

**What did the water say to the boat?**

**Nothing, it just waved.**

**Q:** How is a snail stronger than an elephant?
**A:** Because a snail carries its house on its back, while an elephant only carries its trunk.

**Q:** Why are teddy bears never hungry?
**A:** **Because they are always stuffed.**

**Q:** What gets wet the more it dries?
**A:** **A towel.**

Why are rivers so rich?
Because they have two banks.

What kind of ship never sinks?
Friendship.

I can't believe how much my teacher doesn't know
—she just asks me questions all day!

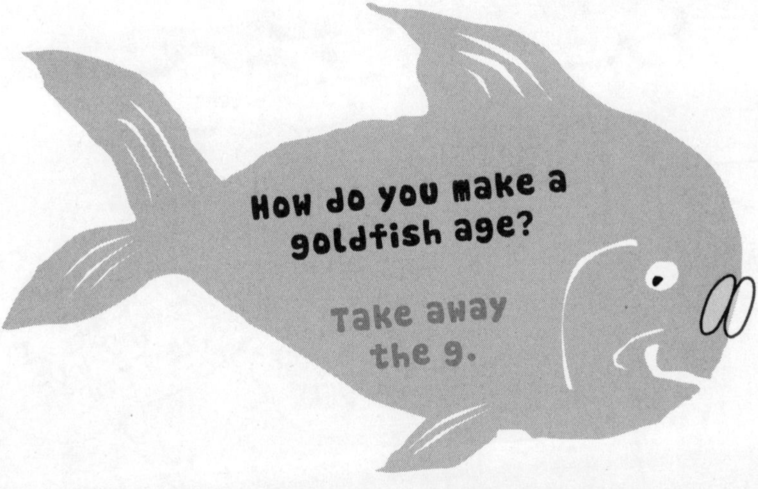

SIR, WOULD YOU PUNISH SOMEONE FOR SOMETHING THEY DIDN'T DO?
OF COURSE NOT.
OH GOOD, BECAUSE I DIDN'T DO MY HOMEWORK.

What do you call a sheep with no legs?
A cloud.

MY DOG PLAYS CHESS.
YOUR DOG PLAYS CHESS? HE MUST BE CLEVER!
NOT REALLY, I WIN MOST OF THE TIME.

Q: Why did the boy bury his torch?
**A: Because the batteries were dead.**

Q: What can you catch but not throw?
**A: A cold.**

Q: What's striped and bouncy?
**A: A tiger on a pogo stick.**

Why are Dalmatians terrible at hide-and-seek?

Because they always get spotted.

Q: Why did the pelican get kicked out of the restaurant? A: Because he had a big bill.

WHY DID THE SKELETON FAIL HIS MATHS TEST?

HIS HEART WAS NOT IN IT.

**What do you get when you cross a hammock and a dog?**

**A rocker spaniel.**

WHAT DID ONE LAPTOP SAY TO THE OTHER LAPTOP?

**Q:** What goes up but never comes down?
**A:** Your age.

Take me out of the box and scratch my head, I am now black but once was red. What am I?

A match.

**Q:** Why couldn't we go to the greengrocer?
**A: There wasn't mushroom.**

HOW DO TREES GET ONLINE?
THEY LOG ON.

**Why are skunks so smart?**
**Because they have a lot of scents!**

Q: Why did the banana factory shut down?
A: Because they chucked out all the bent ones.

I HAVE 400 LEGS AND 5000 ARMS. WHAT AM I?
A LIAR.

Q: What do you call an overweight E.T.?
A: Extra Cholesterol.

# Pick-a-Path

WHY DO BIRDS FLY SOUTH IN THE WINTER?

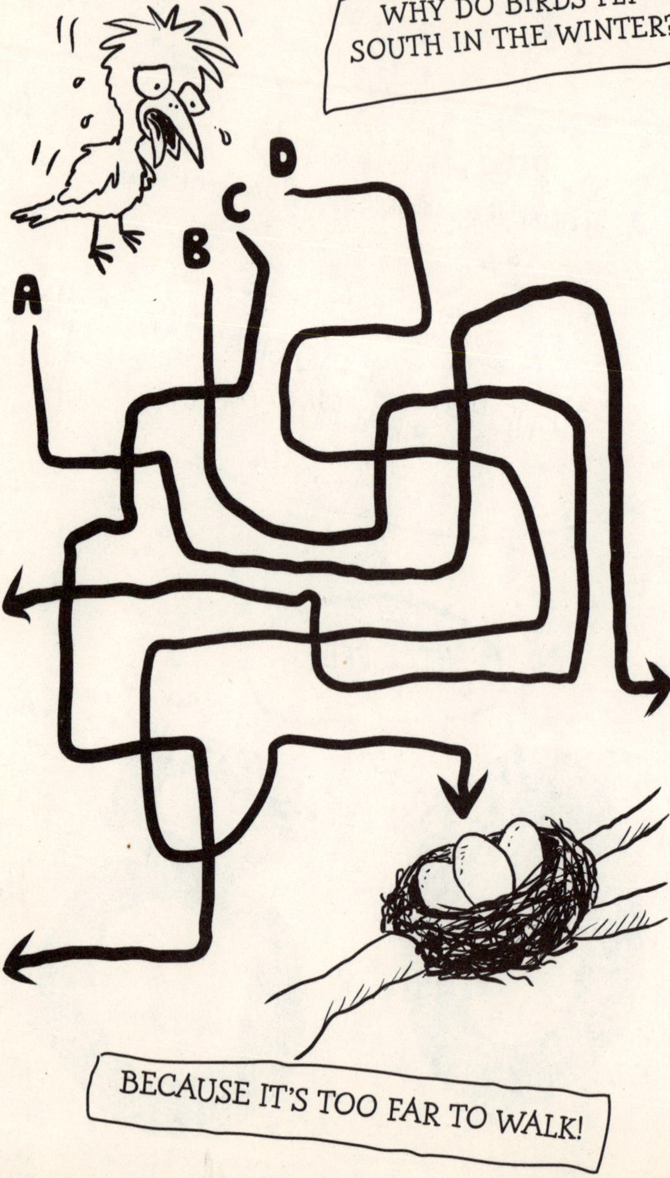


BECAUSE IT'S TOO FAR TO WALK!

**Answer:** Path D

**How do you keep a dumb person in suspense?**
**I'll tell you tomorrow.**

WHAT DO YOU GET WHEN YOU CROSS A COW AND A BELLY DANCER?
**A MILKSHAKE.**

**Q:** How do you make cool music?
**A:** Put your radio in the fridge.

KNOCK, KNOCK!
WHO'S THERE?
KEN.
KEN WHO?
KEN YOU OPEN THE DOOR, PLEASE?

**Q:** Why did the orange stop rolling?
**A:** It ran out of juice.

**Imagine you're in a box.**

**There is no way out.**

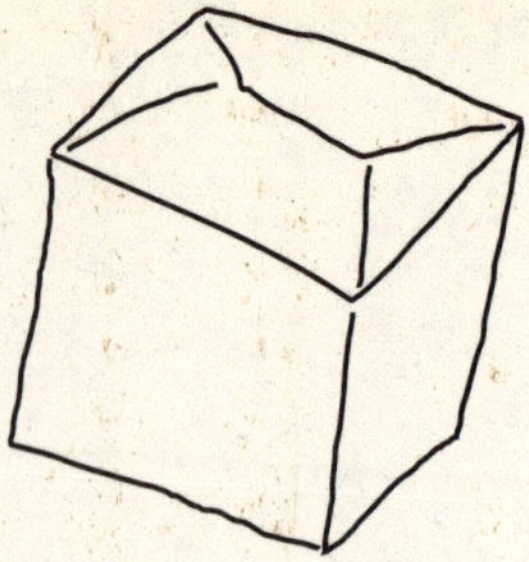

**How do you get out?**

**Stop imagining.**

Q: What's it called when a snowman has a temper tantrum?

A: **A meltdown.**

Q: What doesn't ask questions but must be answered?

A: **A doorbell.**

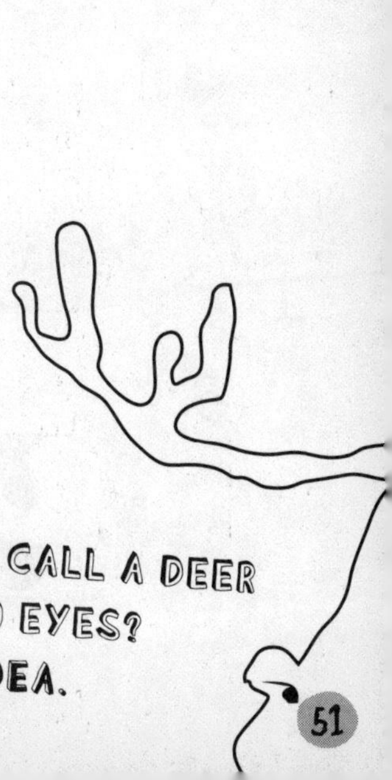

WHAT DO YOU CALL A DEER WITH NO EYES?

NO IDEA.

What goes 'oh, oh, oh'? Santa walking backwards.

Q: What do you call a dinosaur wearing tight shoes?
**A: My-foot-is-saurus.**

Q: When is it bad luck to see a black cat?
**A: When you're a mouse.**

Q: What bird is always out of breath?
A: A puffin.

Why is a tomato round and red?
Because if it was long and green it would be a cucumber.

What do you give a sick lemon? **Lemon aid.**

What happened when the werewolf swallowed a clock? **He got ticks.**

WHAT IS WHITE WHEN IT'S DIRTY AND BLACK WHEN IT'S CLEAN?
A BLACKBOARD.

**What does a kitten become after it is three days old?**
**Four days old.**

Q: As I get older, I become shorter. What am I? **A: A pencil.**

# Crack the Codes

A B C D E F G H I J K L M

N O P Q R S T U V W X Y Z

**Answer:** FRY-DAY and I OVER SWEPT

Why did the tomato blush?
**Because it saw the salad dressing.**

**Knock, knock!**
**Who's there?**
**Sabina.**
**Sabina who?**
**Sabina long time since I've seen you.**

Why did the emu cross the road?
**Because it was the chicken's day off!**

What is easy to get into, but hard to get out of?

Trouble!

Why doesn't the sun go to school?

Because it already has a million degrees.

WHO DID FRANKENSTEIN TAKE TO THE DANCE?

HIS GHOUL FRIEND.

**What do you get when you cross a frog with a rabbit?**
**A bunny ribbit.**

WHAT DO YOU GET WHEN TWO DINOSAURS COLLIDE?

Q: How does a thunderstorm catch fish?
**A: With a lightning rod.**

What did the baby corn say to the mummy corn?
Where's pop corn?

Why wouldn't they let the butterfly into the dance?
Because it was a moth ball.

What animal has more lives than a cat? A frog—he croaks every night!

KNOCK, KNOCK!
**WHO'S THERE?**
JUSTIN.
**JUSTIN WHO?**
JUSTIN TIME FOR DINNER.

Q: Why do fish live in saltwater?
**A: Because pepper water would make them sneeze.**

**What did the mother ghost say to the baby ghost as they drove down the street?**
Buckle your sheet belt.

Why did the plane crash?

Because the pilot was a loaf of bread.

Knock, knock!

Who's there?

Lettuce.

Lettuce who?

Lettuce in!

**What did one toilet say to the other?**
You look a little flushed.

**Q:** Who invented King Arthur's round table?

**A:** Sir Cumference.

HOW DO YOU CUT THE OCEAN IN HALF?
WITH A SEA SAW.

**Q:** What's a toad's favourite sweet?

**A:** Lollihops.

**What do you call cheese that's not yours?**
Nacho cheese.

WHY DIDN'T THE CHICKEN CROSS THE ROAD?
**HE SAW WHAT HAPPENED TO THE ZEBRA.**

# Crazy Creature Mad Lib

One day I found a .............................................................
[colour]

............................................ I decided to keep it and call
[animal]

it .................................................................................. .
[cartoon character]

It was noisy! It sounded like a ......................................... .
[machine]

I showed my ...................................................................
[family member]

and they said '.................................................'.
[sound]

So I took it to school in a ....................................... ,
[object]

but it escaped and ran under a ........................................ .
[object]

My teacher found it and told me to take it straight

to ............................................................................ .
[place]

How do you save a drowning mouse?

**Use mouse to mouse resuscitation.**

**What is in the middle of India?**

**The letter 'd'.**

What button won't you find in a tailor's shop?

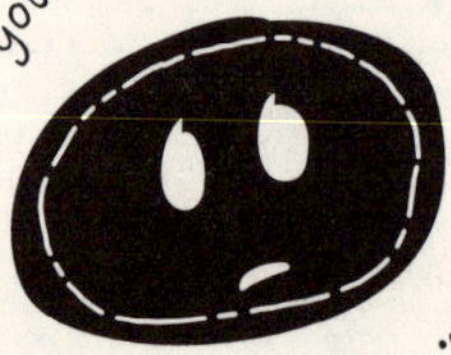

**A belly button.**

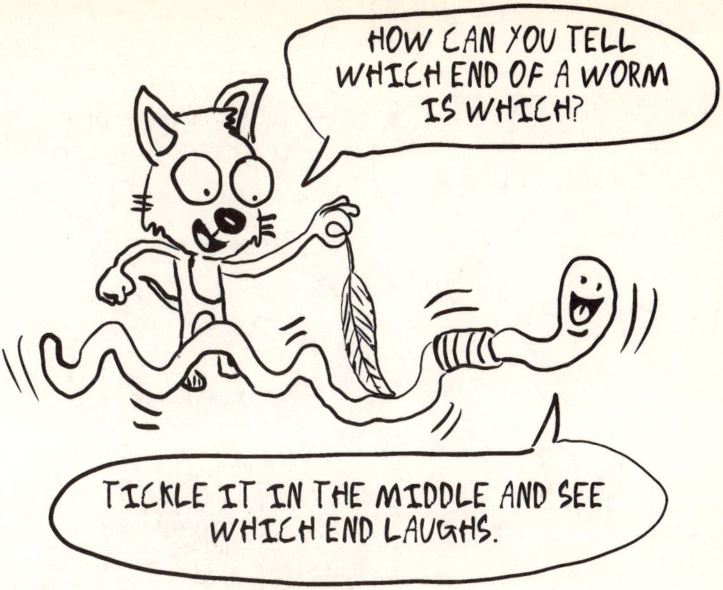

What did the astronaut say when he saw bones on the moon?

**'Obviously the cow didn't make it.'**

WHAT'S THE DIFFERENCE BETWEEN ROAST BEEF AND PEA SOUP?

**EVERYBODY CAN ROAST BEEF BUT NOBODY CAN PEE SOUP!**

WHY DID CAVEMEN DRAW PICTURES OF HIPPOPOTAMUSES AND RHINOCEROSES ON THEIR WALLS?

BECAUSE THEY COULDN'T SPELL THEIR NAMES.

What is full of holes but can still hold water?

A sponge.

Q: Why did the girl stare at the orange juice container for three hours?

A: Because it said concentrate.

**How did the boy feel after he got run over by a car?**
**Tyred.**

Why couldn't the baker buy more bread?

Because he didn't have enough dough.

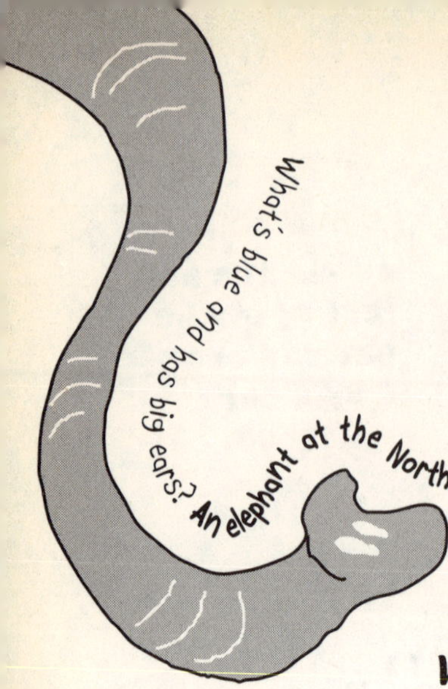

What's blue and has big ears? An elephant at the North pole.

How do you stop a rhino from charging?
Take away its credit card.

What did the policeman say to his belly?
You're under a vest.

What is the strongest vegetable?

A muscle sprout.

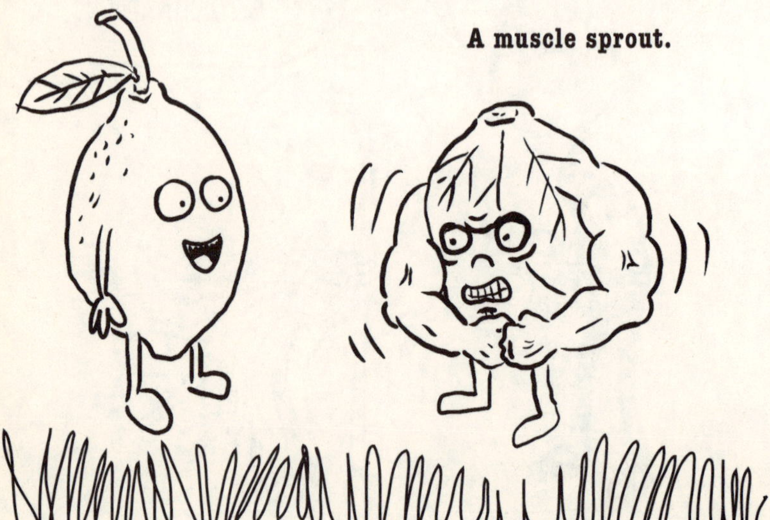

How did the cow cross the road?

He just mooooved across.

What is as big as an elephant but weighs nothing at all?

**Its shadow.**

Q: What do you call a dog with no legs?

**A: It doesn't matter what you call him, he still won't come.**

WHY DID THE BOY ONLY WANT TO DO BACKSTROKE?
HE DIDN'T WANT TO SWIM ON A FULL STOMACH.

Q: How do you stop a dog smelling?
A: Put a peg on its nose.

Q: What do you call a cow with a twitch? A: Beef jerky.

**Why wasn't Cinderella a good soccer player?**
She lost her shoe, she ran away from the ball, and her coach was a pumpkin.

What has two humps and is found at the North Pole?
A lost camel.

**Knock, knock!**
Who's there?
**Amos.**
Amos who?
**A mosquito!**

**What is the most slippery country in the world?**
**Greece.**

HOW DO YOU FEEL WHEN YOU CROSS A SHEEPDOG WITH A MELON?
**MELON-COLLIE.**

What language does a billboard speak?
**Sign language.**

**Q:** What has a bottom at the top?
**A: Your legs.**

**Q:** How did the man call his friend while he was playing in the orchestra?
**A: He used his saxa-phone.**

**WHY DID HALF A CHICKEN CROSS THE ROAD?**
**TO GET TO HIS OTHER SIDE!**

**AN EXHAUSTED KANGAROO.**

Two goldfish are in a tank. One says to the other, 'Do you know how to drive this thing?'

# North Pole Maze

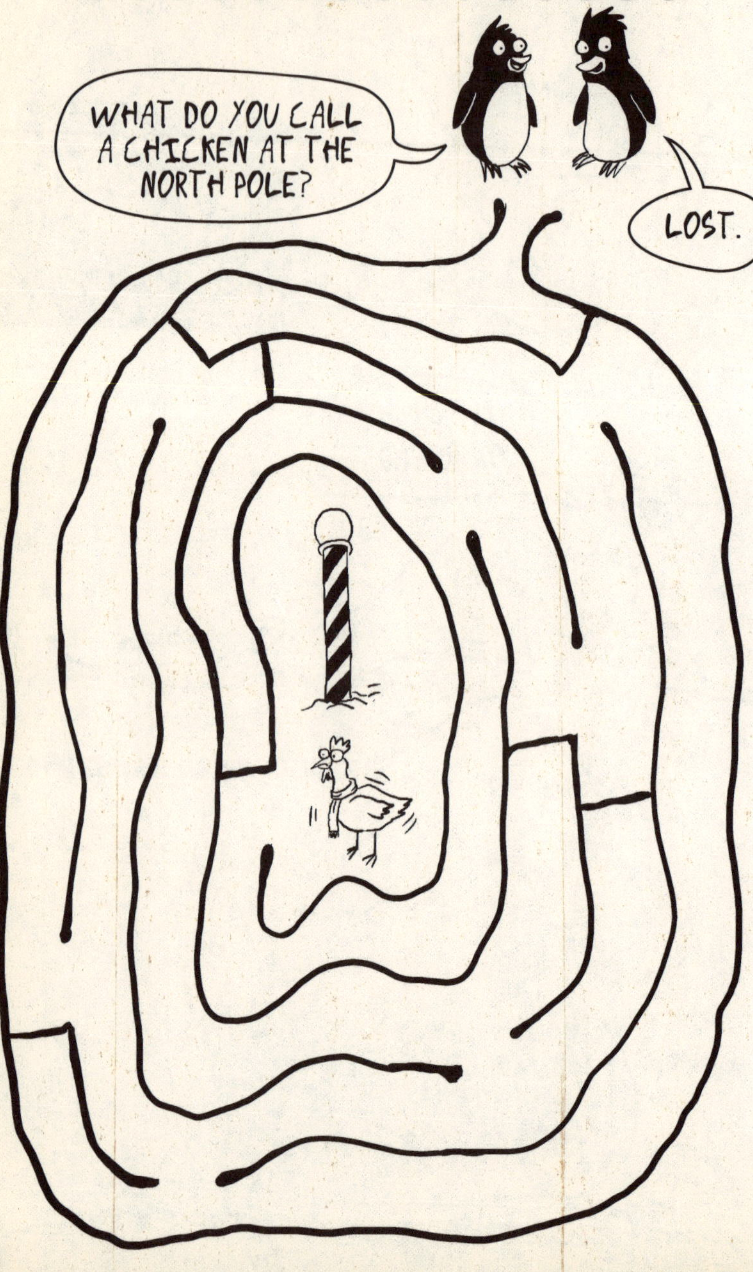

What has forty feet and sings? → The school choir.

What was following the dinosaur? Its tail.

Q: What do you give a sick bird?
A: Tweetment.

Q: There were four cats in a boat, one jumped out. How many were left?
A: None. They were all copy cats.

Why is it so hot at the football field after the game?
Because all the fans have left.

Q: Why did the cow cross the road?
A: To get to the milk bar.

What is a duck's favourite TV show?
The feather forecast.

Why was the computer cold?
**It left its windows open.**

What is grey, but turns red?
**An embarrassed elephant.**

**Q:** Who is the biggest gangster in the sea?
**A:** Al Caprawn.

Why did the silly kid stand on his head?
His feet were tired.

**Two muffins were cooking in the oven. The first muffin said, 'Gosh, it's hot in here!' The second muffin said, 'Aghhh! A talking muffin!'**

**Q:** What do you get from a pampered cow?
**A: Spoiled milk.**

What did Geronimo say when he jumped out of the airplane?
**'ME!!!'**

WHAT DID THE GRAPE DO WHEN IT GOT STEPPED ON?
IT LET OUT A LITTLE WINE.

WHAT DID THE FISH SAY WHEN HE SWAM INTO THE WALL?

**DAM!**

**Why did the house go to the doctor?**

**Because he had window panes.**

Q: Why did the old lady put wheels on her rocking chair?

A: She wanted to rock and roll.

**Q:** What has a head, a tail, and no body?
**A: A coin.**

**Q:** How did the farmer fix his jeans?
**A: With a cabbage patch.**

Why did the vampire brush his teeth?
To stop bat breath.

What is black, white, green and bumpy?
A pickle wearing a tuxedo.

Q: What do you get when you cross a computer and a lifeguard?
A: A screensaver.

Q: Which bird never tells the truth?
A: A lyrebird.

What is a cow's favourite day?

**Moo Year's Day.**

**Why couldn't the athlete listen to her music?**

**Because she broke the record.**

What do lawyers wear to court?

**Lawsuits.**

**Q:** Did you hear the joke about the roof?
**A:** Never mind, it's over your head.

What do you call a witch at the beach?
A sand-witch.

Why did the jellybean go to school?
Because he wanted to be a smartie.

Q: What's the best thing to put into a pie?
**A: Your teeth.**

**What do you get a man who has everything for his birthday?**
**A burglar alarm.**

What did the lawyer name his daughter?
**Sue.**

Why did the witch travel on a broom?

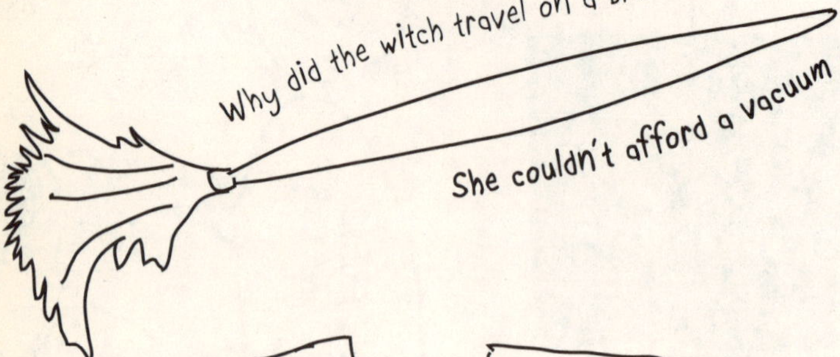

She couldn't afford a vacuum cleaner!

What is the difference between a fly and a bird?
**A bird can fly but a fly can't bird.**

Knock, knock!
**Who's there?**
Bacon.
**Bacon who?**
Bacon a cake for your birthday!

Q: What starts with a P and ends with an E and has a million letters in it?
**A: The Post Office.**

# SPOOKY WORD SEARCH

Find all the words in the puzzle and use the left-over letters to get the answer to the riddle:

WHAT DOES A SHORT-SIGHTED GHOST NEED?

_ _ _ _ _ _ _ _ _ _ _

Z W S P O O K Y M R
O S E P E B O A O E
M M R R O V L O N D
B K A O E I I N S I
I C M E E W E L T P
E A T N R T O A E S
K L H T H C C L R A
C B G G H O S T F L
K C I T S M O O R B
E R N E R I P M A V
F S K E L E T O N S

alien
boo
broomstick
black
cat
evil
frighten
ghost
monster
nightmare
scream
skeleton
spider
spooky
vampire
werewolf
zombie

Answer: SPOOKTACLES

What do you call a single vampire?
A bat-chelor.

Did you hear the joke about the peanut butter?
**I'm not telling you.**
**You might spread it.**

Q: What do you call two banana peels?

**A: A pair of slippers.**

WHAT IS ANOTHER NAME FOR THE MIDDLE AGES?
KNIGHT TIME.

DOCTOR, DOCTOR!
i SWALLOWED A BONE.
ARE YOU CHOKiNG?
NO, i REALLY DiD!

What kind of car does a farmer drive?
A corn-vertible.

Q: What part of a turkey is musical?
A: The drumstick.

Q: Why do bees have sticky hair?
A: Because they use honey combs!

**Q:** Why did the cat run away from the tree?
**A:** It was afraid of the bark!

**WHY ARE VAMPIRES TOUGH TO GET ALONG WITH?**
BECAUSE THEY CAN BE PAINS IN THE NECK.

WHERE DID THE MUSIC TEACHER LEAVE HIS KEYS?
**ON THE PIANO.**

Q: Why did the farmer ride his horse to town?

A: It was too heavy to carry.

WHAT'S THE DIFFERENCE BETWEEN A TV AND A NEWSPAPER?

EVER TRIED SWATTING A FLY WITH A TV?

What do you do if you break your toe?

Call a toe truck.

The ringmaster tripped over a giraffe and shouted, 'You can't keep that lying there!' The keeper said, 'Sir, that's not a lion, it's a giraffe.'

What is the best way to catch a fish?
Have someone throw it at you.

Why did the man run around his bed? To catch up on his sleep.

What is green and has yellow wheels?
Grass . . . I lied about the wheels.

Q: What did one tonsil say to the other tonsil?
A: 'Get dressed, the doctor is taking us out tonight.'

What did the alien say to the garden?
Take me to your weeder.

WHAT DO SKATEBOARDS EAT FOR LUNCH?
ROLLS.

**WHAT DO YOU DO IF YOUR UNICYCLE GETS A FLAT TYRE?**

# Joke-a-thon Winners!

**Will Sugden, VIC**

Joke-a-thon Winner!

**Where do witches learn to fly?**

**Broome!**

**Lisa Mainwaring, NSW**

Joke-a-thon Runner-Up

**What did the young shrimp say to his mum when he wasn't sharing his toys?**

**Sorry, I'm a little shellfish.**

**Ryan Cox, NSW**

Joke-a-thon Runner-Up

camp quality.

laughter is the best medicine.

With special thanks to contributors and supporters!

Thank you to all who helped with this book, for all your hilarious jokes and support. A special thank you to the many Australian children, celebrities and public for your contributions.

Taylor
Gus White
Kiarak Hibberson
Beth Gleeson
Reef
Giselle Varricchio
Era Nyman
Hannah Page
Jacob Mayr
Liam Sims
Riley Wiseman
Joshua Eggleton
Lauren Bailey
Kayla Stewart
Samara Louise Balcombe
James Peters
Daniel Mitchell
Ellie Williams
Kimberly Mitchell
Peter Zabala

Ryan Cox
Ella
Ben Schley
Thomas Gerlach
Joel
Zacharie Cook
Daymon Tuthill Ayesha Dean
Macey Bird
Portia Crawford
Binil Kunnummaliyil Scaria
Mason Mancuso
Tahlia Inkster
Maya Nair
Mattheus Galjaardt
Jade Kember
Dakota
Lucius Beh
Lucas Adcock
Lisa Mainwaring
Will Sugden

camp quality.

laughter is the best medicine.

Have you got a funny joke?
Send it to us and it might just end up being published in next year's joke book.
How cool would that be?

Send it to us online now **campquality.org.au/yourjoke** or write it down and post it.

**Camp Quality**
**My Joke**
**PO Box 400**
**Epping NSW 1710**

Name .............................................. Age ..............

Address ..............................................................

..............................................................

State .............................................. Postcode ..............

Phone ..............................................................

Email ..............................................................

My cool joke! ..............................................................

..............................................................

..............................................................

# You can help!

Your gift will help Camp Quality continue to reach out to children and their families facing cancer this year.
Donate to your local CQ online
campquality.org.au
or post the slip below.

## Yes, I want to help create a better life for children living with cancer in Australia!
'Thanks so much for your kind support.'

My gift amount is: (please tick)

☐ $25 ☐ $50 ☐ Other ................

Gift Frequency: ☐ One-off ☐ Monthly

My details are:

Title: ..... First name: .............. Surname: ..............................

Address: ..................................................................

Suburb/Town: ............................ State: .... Postcode: ............

Phone/Mobile: ..............................................................

Email: .....................................................................

I wish to make my payment by:

☐ Cheque / Money Order ☐ Mastercard ☐ Visa ☐ Amex

Card number: ☐☐☐☐ ☐☐☐☐ ☐☐☐☐ ☐☐☐☐

Expiry: ☐☐ / ☐☐ Name on card: ..............................

Your signature: .................... Today's date: ........................

Please return this completed form to: Camp Quality, Reply Paid 400, Epping NSW 1710 or fax (02) 9869 0688 or call (02) 9876 0500 or donate online at mycampquality.org.au/donate or email donorcare@campquality.org.au
All donations over $2 are tax deductible.
ABN 87 052 097 720